CREATE PASSIVE

INCOME

STRATEGIES FOR FINANCIAL INCREASE

CREATE PASSIVE

INCOME

STRATEGIES FOR FINANCIAL INCREASE

from the author of

The 21 Day Empowerment Factor

and

Life, Vision, Purpose

DR. DEBRA WRIGHT OWENS

Copyright © 2023, 2022 by Debra Wright Owens

All rights reserved. Printed in the United States of America. No part of this publication may be reproduced, stored in a retrieval system, or transmitted in any form or by any means, electronic, mechanical, photocopying, recording, or otherwise, without the written consent of the author.

Written by Dr. Debra Wright Owens

Encore Empowerment International, LLC
Dallas, GA 30132

Cover design by Marius Owens and Debra Wright Owens.

ISBN - 9798867300548

Dedication

I would like to dedicate **Create Passive Income: Strategies for Financial Increase** to my daughter Jasmin, my son Marius, my family, friends and those of you around the world, who are in pursuit of your God-given purpose.

"None of us will make it out of here alive. In the meantime, LIVE!" -Myesha Chaney

ACKNOWLEDGEMENTS

All praises and honor to God the most-High, for imparting the idea in me to write *"Create Passive Income: Strategies for Financial Increase"*. I am grateful for each and every creative idea that is downloaded into my mind and the ongoing opportunity to inform, inspire and empower others to do, be and say "more". We are all created by the Creator, to be Creative!

I thank my children (Jasmin and Marius) who continuously inspire me to do more, and always bring me joy. Thank you for your love, patience, encouragement and support. Thank you for believing in me and cheering me on continuously, through the highs and lows and all my creative endeavors. I am thankful to my family and friends for their ongoing support. You all have helped me to continue striving for all things excellent as I continue to chart my life's journey.

I am grateful for my team members who helped me put this e-book together and make it available to you.

Introduction

The world is full of positive and productive opportunities. You can see them all around if you stop long enough to *bask in the beauty of life*. These many opportunities also come with hidden treasures in them. That hidden treasure can be labeled as many things. One person may find peace in an opportunity. Another may find joy in an opportunity. While another may find the answer to a problem in an opportunity. Then there are those who are looking for opportunities that pay – PAY MONEY THAT IS! Peace, joy, answers and money are all treasures! Perhaps what you find in the opportunities you come across, depends largely on what you are actually looking for in life.

Money is something that we all can use, and truthfully, we can never have too much of it. If by chance you think that you have too much money, then by all means be generous and give to a worthy cause. Money is the currency by which we transact the sale and purchase of goods and services daily. Even if we can't visibly see the daily transactions, trust me that they are happening behind the scenes in some way or another. Money is generally earned by working a "9 to 5" job for it; eight hours a day – five days a week, and is also referred to as income or earned income. ***Income can be active or passive***. Most people have an active income stream, such as from a job (as I mentioned above), where there is a direct connection between the work you perform daily and the pay you receive in return for performing that work. With passive income, the connection is not so obvious, at least from the perspective of working daily at a task to receive payment for it in return. However, there is still work that goes into generating passive income. The work that is connected to passive income generally takes place upfront, and the income generates afterwards.

Many people are now pursuing passive income streams to supplement their active income. The plight of passive income has sort of become the *new normal* with earning income, especially in light of skyrocketing prices due to inflation. Ideas and opportunities for generating passive income are also on the rise, and people are literally making more money in their sleep. The benefits of generating passive income include financial security, debt relief, schedule and time flexibility, work-life balance, allowance for goal(s) achievement, location independence, reduced stress and early retirement. Generating passive income may very well be the opportunity that you have been waiting for to catapult you to living your dream life!

CREATE PASSIVE

INCOME

STRATEGIES FOR FINANCIAL INCREASE

CONTENTS

Build Wealth Through Creativity

A Definition for Passive Income?

Any income other than regular earnings from an employer or contractor, can be considered Passive income. According to the Internal Revenue Service, passive income can be sourced from such things as rental property, hobbies, or even stock investments. Passive income is one of the best ways to earn more money, and design the life that you truly desire.

While passive income does not involve hands-down nonstop 9-5 work, it does involve a level of work periodically and possibly a small investment, at least to get things started. For example, if you desire to create income from stock investments, you would have to set up a stock account, and make initial and periodic investments to gain dividend returns (to create a continuous stream of passive income). You can reap a great return from any initial investment that you make starting out. Whether you looking for more financial security or stability, creating a passive income stream is a great way to start.

10 ideas for creating passive income

Here are 10 ideas to create passive income, and establish financial stability, security and wealth! See what these ideas entail, what it takes to get started, and some estimates of how much passive income you can generate from these ideas.

1

Create A Course

1. Create a course

Course creation has become a high-end, high-ticket trend in the passive income industry. Actually, it has become a trend in the regular income industry as well. But for purposes of this E-book, we will look at creating a course as an idea for passive income. If you possess expert knowledge on a topic or in particular field, you may consider sharing that knowledge to help others and create passive income while doing so. A course can be created in audio or video format, or a combination of both.

There are many course creation platforms available now, and the prices vary for use of these platforms to build your course on. You can explore your options, considering such factors as your budget, target audience, course topic, course value to students, etc. Once you have decided on your course topic, and the course builder platform that you will build on, then you can move forward with building your course. After your course has been built, you will need to decide on your branding, marketing, promoting, and the price that you will charge for your course.

Your course can be sold through your individual website or you can sell and distribute your course through a third-party platform such Udemy, Skillshare and Coursera. There are advantages and challenges with each option. For example, if you sell on your own website, you get 100% of the profits. On the other hand, if you sell your course on a third-party website such as Udemy, your exposure to customers will be huge, but your course price per sale will be much lower. The great thing is, you get to decide?

Here are a few course builder platforms for your reference:

- Thinkific
- Teachable
- LearnWorlds
- Udemy
- SkillShare
- Ruzuku
- Academy Of Mine
- WizIQ
- Kajabi
- Moodle

Creating a course can be an excellent passive income stream, because once you have done the upfront work to build it, distribute it, and promote it – it constantly pays you. However, your course needs to be much more than an average course. Aim for excellence so you can make good money from it.

Let's Calculate the Passive Income:

Example

Sell a course on your website at $100/sale x 100/sales = $10,000 (passive income)

Sell a course on your website at $29/sale x 100/sales = $2900 (passive income)

Sell a course on a 3rd party platform at $29/sale x 100/sales x 50% commission = $1450 (passive income)

2

Write An E-Book

2. Write an e-book

Writing and publishing e-books is another popular trend that has literally skyrocketed over the last several years and is also an excellent idea for creating passive income. With advancements in technology, anyone can self-publish an e-book. An e-book can be created as a Microsoft Word document, saved as a PDF file and made available on your website or other digital download platforms for payment. Your e-book can also be published and distributed through Kindle Direct Publishing, which would allow you to leverage its worldwide customer base and earn a continuous royalties "passive income" stipend for each sale. The percentage of royalties you earn on an e-book varies depending on the publisher. You would need to explore different publishers, weigh your options, and decide which publisher to go with.

E-books can range from 30-50 pages on average and have relative low-cost to create. Remember, you are creating the e-book from your expert knowledge on a given topic or field. E-books can be designed quickly, to include cover art, formatting and downloading options. Canva is a great resource for creating e-books and it offers both cover art and e-book design templates.

You can conduct market research to gain insight on price points for your e-book, and decide on a price based on your research results, the upfront work you put in to create the e-book, and the content value. The amount of passive income you can generate from writing and publishing an e-book depends on you and your marketing strategies. Once you have written and published your e-book, on your website or a 3rd party platform, it's out there in the cyber-tech world to generate passive income for you.

Of course, your e-book needs to be better than average to gain traction and create a constant stream of passive income. Aim to create and deliver value, and your customer base will help you spread the word and promote your e-book. If you put minimum effort into creating your e-book, then don't expect to gain a harvest in return.

Here are a few e-book publishing platforms for your reference:

- Kindle Direct Publishing
- Kobo Writing Life
- Smashwords
- Draft2Digital
- Lulu
- Barnes & Noble Press

Let's Calculate the Passive Income:

Example

Sell an e-book on your website at $10/sale x 100/sales = $1,000 (passive income)

Sell an e-book on your website at $19/sale x 50/sales = $950 (passive income)

Sell an e-book on a 3rd party publishing platform at $10/sale x 100/sales x 20% royalty = $200 (passive income)

3

Paid Membership Site

3. Start a Paid Membership Website

A paid membership site is a private site that you can create and add new content to on a regular basis. Access to the content is given to people who subscribe to the membership site and pay a monthly fee. The monthly fee can range from $5-$200 (or more) per month, depending on the offerings and depth of content. Some content on the membership site may be given for free to potential subscribers as a marketing strategy, to give them an idea of what's available, in hopes that they will subscribe and pay a monthly membership fee to get more content.

To create a paid membership website, you should consider such factors as 1) defining your ideal member and target market, 2) testing your membership site idea, 3) pricing your membership site monthly fee, 4) designing your membership website, 5) creating your membership site content, and 6) building your membership site community. Creating and starting a paid membership website is not for the faint at heart. It takes upfront work, which many prefer not to endure. If you're up for the challenge, the rewards of recurring passive income are well worth it.

Here are a few paid membership website ideas for your reference:

- Cooking and recipes
- Photo and video editing

- Coaching
- Auctions
- Business and marketing training
- Computer coding
- Health and fitness
- Web design

Let's Calculate the Passive Income:

Example

100/subscribers x $10/monthly subscription fee = $1,000 (passive income)

20/subscribers x $100/premium monthly subscription = $2000 (passive income)

10/subscribers x $250/premium monthly subscription = $2500 (passive income)

4

Rental Income

4. Rental income

Rental property investing is an ever-growing passive income source. It generally requires more work than many other passive income sources, but the returns have shown to be greater also. Before charting the rental property investing territory, it is highly recommended that you do your background research, to ensure you don't overlook anything that could cause you to lose out on more than you put in. Many people have reported huge success with using rental property investing to create passive income, and have used their knowledge of the niche to teach others the same.

When exploring the idea of rental property investing as a source of passive income, you should consider such things as 1) the amount you want to invest on the property, 2) how much return you want on your investment, 3) the expenses associated with owning the property, and 4) any financial risks associated with owning the property (such as economic downturns, inflation, damages to the property, etc.). It's a good idea to give careful thought to these factors, before making a final decision to proceed with investing in rental property.

Here are a few rental property investment ideas for your reference:

- Retail space
- Office space

- Parking space
- Residential space
- Fixer-uppers

Let's Calculate the Passive Income:

Example

$1700/monthly rental fee - $1100/monthly PITI = $600 (passive income)

$2400/monthly rental fee - $1500/monthly PITI = $900 (passive income)

$1000/month rental fee - $600/monthly PITI = $400 (passive income)

5

Book Anthology Project

5. Launch a Book Anthology Project

Writing and launching a book anthology project can yield a huge and immediate passive income injection. The book anthology trend has taken the writing and publishing industry to by storm and to new heights. In days of old, writing a book was viewed as a very tedious and intimidating journey, that only the brave at heart dared to pursue. Those brave hearts had to pursue and obtain approval of their manuscript from the founding publishing companies, before they could proceed with writing a book.

Advance technology has changed the narrative of book writing and publishing. Not only can you write and self-publish a book as a solo author, you can now write and self-publish a book anthology featuring many contributing authors – allowing them all to share their story or message in the same place at the same time.

The steps to writing, self-publishing and launching your very own book anthology can appear to be challenging, but once you have done your research or actually have prior experience with completing one or participating in one, it doesn't come across as intimidating anymore. Before pressing the green light to get started, you will need to decide on the topic for your book anthology. Then you will need to pursue your target contributing authors by announcing a "call for authors" and holding an informational session for those who have expressed an interest in your project. Of course there are more steps to the big picture afterwards, but I wanted to share with you how to get started. A book anthology project can span 3 to 4 months from start to launch, and the price for contributing authors can range from $97-$1500 (or more depending on the visionary author's market influence).

If you don't know already, you are probably wandering how passive income can be created from a book anthology. Trust me, you can create passive income from a book anthology. As the visionary author, you decide how much money you want to make from the anthology project, how often you want to have a passive income injection from a book anthology, the price you will charge each contributing author to be a part of the anthology, and the number of contributing authors you will need to reach your goal.

There will be expenses associated with getting your book anthology created, such as cover art design, graphic promotions for the contributing authors, editing/publishing and marketing ads, etc. Once the expenses are cleared, you will have a reasonable passive income net profit. The reward is not only the passive income injection, but also the opportunity you have extended to others to share their story and message and become an author.

Here are a few book anthology topic ideas for your reference:

- Cooking and recipes
- Motivation messages
- Empowerment and self-help
- Single parenting
- Co-parenting
- Entrepreneurship
- Studying abroad
- Overcoming setbacks
- Spiritual messages
- Affirmations and poems

Let's Calculate the Passive Income:

Example

30/contributing authors x $97/contributor fee = $2910 (passive income)

20/contributing authors x $297/contributor fee = $5940 (passive income)

40/contributing authors x $197/contributor fee = $7800 (passive income)

30/contributing authors x $1200/contributor fee = $36,000 (passive income)

6

Room or House Rental

6. Rent Out a Room in Your House or Apartment

Many have opted to rent out a room in their home to create passive income. This is a popular trend for those who want to generate passive income in addition to what they earn on their 9-5 job, as well as for those who are looking to share rental/mortgage expenses. Some have even gone as far as to rent out several rooms in their home to maximize their passive income generating potential.

If you have extra space, feel safe with doing so, and are open to embracing different personalities, then this might just be the route for you to take and create a passive income stream. For example, if you are leasing a three-bedroom apartment and you live alone, you could rent out the other two bedrooms at a rate that would totally cover or almost cover your monthly rental rate. If you own a three-bedroom home, you could do the same. You could even include meals for an additional fee, if you like to cook. You could really be creative with this idea. Renting a room in your apartment or house, can range anywhere between $50-$90 per night or $400-$800 per month. It depends on location, amenities, and of course the renter's need.

If you decide to go this route and rent out a room in your apartment or home, the process is not that difficult. You would need to explore rental platform options to list your space on, such as Airbnb. There are several platforms to choose from, that are more advanced than the older tradition of listing a "room for rent" in the local newspaper. At the click of a button, these platforms will connect you with people who are looking to rent space. Haven't we come so far?

Of course, upfront work on your part is required to get your space ready for listing and promoting, but if your space "wows" potential renters, you should have no problems with making a passive income return on your upfront work and investment.

Here are a few room and space rental platforms ideas for reference:

- Airbnb
- Apartments.com
- RentoMeter
- PadSplit
- VRBO
- Booking.com

Let's Calculate the Passive Income:

Example

$50/nightly room rental rate x 12/nights per month = $600 (passive income)

$70/nightly room rental rate x 10/nights per month = $700 (passive income)

$600/monthly room rental rate x 3/months = $1800 (passive income)

$500/monthly room rental rate x 6/months = $3000 (passive income)

$800/monthly room rental rate x 12/months = $9600 (passive income)

7

Custom Graphic Designs

7. Sell custom graphic designs online

E-commerce has paved the way for creating and selling custom graphic designs online, and made it possible to generate passive income for anyone who desires to do so. If you possess graphic design skills and have an eye for artsy creativity, then you may very well have a competitive edge with creating passive income in this lane. You can literally turn your creative graphical visions into passive income profits. You can even promote your services to design for events, companies and others, from their visions.

Businesses such as Teespring, CafePress and Zazzle allow graphic creatives to promote and sell custom products on their platforms. If you decide to create a storefront and sell on these platforms, not only can you save on upfront inventory ordering expenses and glean from their huge customer base, you can also benefit from the print and ship on demand features that they offer and build your own product brand. If you decide to order inventory upfront and sell your designs on your own website, such as on the Shopify platform, you will have to do more work promoting yourself. Whether you want to design and create t-shirts, hats, mugs, cupholders, or hoodies, it is up to you – you decide.

To get started with selling graphic designs online, you can simply decide on the graphic design genres that you want to pursue (from your own creativity or for others), explore the different online graphic design platforms – considering whether their features match your needs, weigh the pros and cons of going with a design platform versus your own website, make a decision on the route you will take, then start designing and promoting your designs for sell. With a few minor processes to put in place here and there, you can be in business right away and create passive income. If your design skills can set you apart from the rest, the competition in this lane can be a nonfactor because the odds of someone else creating the same design idea would be minimal.

Here are a few online graphic design platform ideas for reference:

- Teespring
- Zazzle
- CafePress
- Printful
- Vistaprint
- Shopify

Let's Calculate the Passive Income:

Example

20/t-shirt sales for small event x $25/per t-shirt from stocked inventory = $500 (passive income)

40/hat sales for a small business x $10/per hat from stocked inventory = $400 (passive income)

50/mug sales from you online storefront x $10/per mug = $500 (passive income)

8

Digital Product Downloads

8. Create and sell digital products

Digital product downloads are now a dime a dozen. They are digital files such as audiobooks, PDFs, templates, plug-ins, or e-books that you can download at the click of button from your computer. Not only are they convenient, most are hassle-free and provide for a great customer experience. There are no inventory or storage costs associated with digital products, so their passive income margins are relatively high. You can create a digital product one time, and sell that same digital product a thousand times over to create a passive income stream. There is no cap on the number of digital download copies you can sell.

Creating and selling digital products can be a lucrative passive income generator. You can automate the entire process, have it made available to a global customer base, and make passive income from your digital products while you sleep or while you are swinging the club on the golf course!

There are many online services that make selling your digital products easy, such as Sellfy and Podia. You would have to create an account with these platforms to sell your digital downloads on their website. You can even create a PayPal button on your website to sell your digital product downloads. The decision on which platform to sell on is totally yours. The most work involved with selling digital products, is creating them. Once they have been created, they can be considered *"gifts that keep on giving"*.

Here are a few digital download platform ideas for reference:

- Gumroad
- Teachable
- Sellfy
- Payhip
- Podia
- Sellwire
- FlickRocket
- DPD (*Digital Product Delivery*)

Let's Calculate the Passive Income:

Example

$5/digital "how to" guide x 200/downloads per month = $1000 (passive income)

$12/digital audio book x 100/downloads per month = $1200 (passive income)

$7/digital PDF white paper x 50/downloads per month = $350 (passive income)

$29/digital course x 50/downloads per month = $1450 (passive income)

9

Create & Sell Greeting Cards

9. Create & Sell Greeting Cards

Creating greeting cards can be a rewarding passive income stream. You can create greeting cards for many different occasions, including holidays, birthdays, graduations, promotions, and other special occasions. You can sell your greeting cards directly to your customer base from your own website, sell them to wholesale or retail stationary companies – who will sell them to customers, sell them via a shop or in a mall kiosk. You get to decide how you create and sell your greeting cards. Research and explore which options best fits you.

If you decide to pursue creating and selling greeting cards to generate passive income, bear in mind that "your designs matter". Aim for the stars and design high quality greeting cards, in graphics and content. Remember, you want the customer base to experience what your cards express.

Getting started is fairly simple. You would need to decide on graphic designs, themes, paper stock and envelops, printing, etc. Seek out specialty printing companies to get your cards printed up; those that offer such choices as elite card fabrics, glitter, foiling, etc. Even look for specialty envelopes. If you don't have a creative design background, you can have someone else create the designs for your greeting cards. Fiverr is a great resource for getting graphic design jobs done. They offer hundreds to thousands of designers to choose from.

As you are probably aware, the price for greeting cards can range from $.99-$7.99 each from a retailor. The price for a box of holiday themed greeting cards, such as Christmas cards, can range from $3-$15. This should give you an idea of the amount of passive income that is possible from creating and selling greeting cards. A small home-based greeting card business can make up to $15,000 in passive income per year, if that is the goal amount. We know that large companies like Hallmark, make billions of dollars selling special occasion greeting cards. Again, it is all up to you!

Here are a few platform ideas to sell greeting cards for your reference:

- Amazon
- Etsy
- eBay
- ArtFire
- Shopify
- iCraft
- Hallmark

Let's Calculate the Passive Income:

Example

$2/greeting card x 300/sales per month = $600 (passive income)

$3/greeting card x 100/sales per month = $300 (passive income)

$5/pack of 15 greeting cards x 100/sales per month = $500 (passive income)

10

Online Tutoring Service

10. Start an online tutoring service

Creating and operating an online tutoring service can generate passive income and eventually grow into a full-time income. This is a booming business market, that's in demand now. Not only does a tutoring side hustle help students reach their learning and academic goals, it can also expand your teaching expertise and place you in another income bracket. Starting your own online tutoring service has little to no start-up costs, especially if you already have a home office, are familiar with marketing and promoting trends, and currently possess the subject matter expert knowledge that you will be tutoring on.

Before starting out, you'll need to consider such factors as your ideal client or target market (what grade levels you will tutor), whether you will conduct 1:1 or group tutoring. Some clients may prefer 1:1 tutoring, which focuses on the specific strengths and weakness of an individual student. On the other hand, some clients may prefer group tutoring, which can create an interactive "team" environment, encourages creative thinking and strengthens communication skills.

You would also need to consider other factors, such as the hours you will tutor, how you will promote your tutoring services, and of course how you will price your services. Afterall, creating a stream of passive income is one objective of starting an online tutoring service.

An online tutoring service can create passive income up to $40,000 year, depending on the rates you charge and how much you work. On average, tutoring service hourly rates are along the lines of $22. As you can see from these numbers, an online tutoring service can create a very rewarding passive income. Again, it's all up to you! You decide how much passive income you want to make.

Here are a few tutoring niche ideas to consider for your reference:

- Specialist tutors
- Pre-K tutors
- Basic and elementary math
- Test prep tutors (ACT, SAT, CLEP, GRE, GMAT, etc.)
- Language and ESL tutors
- Admissions and applications tutors
- College/University tutors
- Calculus
- Chemistry
- Physics

Let's Calculate the Passive Income:

Example

$50/specialist tutoring hourly rate x 40/online hours per month = $2000 (passive income)

$15/elementary math tutoring hourly rate x 32/online hours per = $480 (passive income)

$35/test prep hourly rate x 16/sales per month = $560 (passive income)

Deciding which passive income idea is best?

The passive income ideas featured in this e-book are just a few to get your creative thought process turning. These ideas are for individuals looking to supplement their existing income passively, as well as those with a no income starting point. This list is by no means "the list" or "the law", neither is it exhaustive. There are so many more ideas in existence to choose from. The calculation examples included in this e-book are *examples only*, provided to give you an idea of how much passive income you could generate. No two "real time" scenarios would yield identical results, as there are different factors to consider in each scenario. Hopefully, you get the point intended.

Deciding which passive income strategy is best for you, depends on several factors. One prevalent factor is your passive income goal. That will more than likely be the starting point or fuel by which subsequent factors will be guided. You will also need to consider other factors such as the upfront investment, the market demand, your competition, your knowledge, experience and abilities, and your potential to succeed. Weighing passive income opportunities against such factors as these, can help you decide which passive income strategy would be most beneficial to you and your goals.

How many passive income streams should I have?

It's all up to you and your goals. The sky is the limit and you are the captain of your ship. If you want to create only one passive income stream, that's fine. If you want to create multiple passive income streams, that's fine too. There is no "*golden rule*" that establishes a concrete number. If you have a need, desire, knowledge, time and talent – then by all means go for it! Why not share your strengths with others, and generate passive income while doing so? Just make sure you don't take on more than you can handle, lose focus, and offer services beneath the spirit of excellence. Remember, your efforts and work should be customer and client-centered also, and not only passive income driven. After all, your customers and clients will be the individuals who pay you for your time and services!

Conclusion

Creating passive income streams can set you up for financial security. There are no limits on the amount of passive income you can create, unlike a 9-5 salary that an employer pays you. Many benefits are associated with creating passive income streams, to include scheduling flexibilities, tax benefits, financial independence, and debt relief – just to name a few. Your customers and clients also benefit from the services you provide. If you want to create passive income, then why not start today!

Before getting started on your passive income journey, be sure to research the requirements for starting a business in your state and county. Most Secretary of State offices and county business offices have helpful resources that guide you through the process of setting up and registering your business as a legal entity, step-by-step (if needed). Make sure that if you're going to be in business to make passive income, then do business the right way so you can reap the greatest rewards.

Resourceful Links

Create a Course resources

https://www.thinkific.com/

https://teachable.com/

https://www.learnworlds.com/

https://www.udemy.com/

https://www.skillshare.com/

https://www.ruzuku.com/

https://www.academyofmine.com/

https://www.wiziq.com/

https://kajabi.com/

https://moodle.org/

Write an E-book resources

https://kdp.amazon.com/en_US/

https://www.kobo.com/us/en/p/writinglife

https://www.smashwords.com/

https://www.draft2digital.com/

https://www.lulu.com/

https://press.barnesandnoble.com/

Room or House Rental resources

https://www.airbnb.com/

https://www.apartments.com/

https://www.rentometer.com/

https://www.padsplit.com/

https://www.vrbo.com/

https://www.booking.com/

Custom Graphic Designs resources

https://teespring.com/

https://www.zazzle.com/

https://www.cafepress.com/

https://www.printful.com/

https://www.vistaprint.com/

https://www.shopify.com/

Digital Product Downloads resources

https://gumroad.com/

https://sellfy.com/

https://payhip.com/

https://www.podia.com/

https://sellwire.net/

https://www.flickrocket.com/en/

https://getdpd.com/

Greeting Card resources

https://artfire.com/

https://icraftgifts.com/

https://www.hallmark.com/

Meet the Author

Dr. Debra Wright Owens is an Executive Leadership Coach, best-selling Author, Speaker and Minister, whose been gifted by God to Inspire, Inform, and EMPOWER individuals to maximize their potential and be successful in their lane, on their terms. She is founder of Encore Empowerment International, LLC a professional service firm that specializes in top tier business solutions, training and development and conflict resolution (arbitration and mediation). She also founded The Visionaire Foundation, Inc. (non-profit organization), a global visionary movement dedicated to enhancing the lives of others through knowledge and selfless service. Dr. Owens possesses a unique ability to get to the CORE of the matter, and is committed to empowering individuals to bridge the gap between their "vision & reality", and get on track to LIVE the life that they truly desire to live - on purpose!

She has over 33 years of professional career experience in federal sector corporate America, to include being a military veteran, where she served in management and leadership capacity -mentoring, coaching, and advising others. She has earned certifications in professional coaching, facilitative instruction, grant writing, performance accountability, business entrepreneurship, mediation and arbitration - to name a few. She also holds a PhD in Business Administration and a Master in Public Administration. Her natural and professional abilities and skillset combined, fully equips her to serve and help others grow, as well as set them on the path to living vision and purpose!

By far, her greatest accomplishment is being mother to her two angels, Jasmin and Marius! They are truly gifts that keep on giving. When she's not informing, inspiring and empowering others to do and be MORE, you can find her exploring the world through reading and research, hidden behind the pages of a good book, perfecting a great recipe or nurturing her future billionaire philanthropic ambitions.

Dr. Debra Wright Owens' contact info:

Founder/CEO
ENCORE Empowerment International, LLC
http://www.encoreempowermentint.com and
The VISIONAIRE FOUNDATION, Inc.
www.visionairefoundationinc.org

Follow me *https://linktr.ee/Dr.DebraWrightOwens*
Connect on *https://www.facebook.com/debra.wrightowens/*
Connect on LinkedIn *www.linkedin.com/in/dr-debra-wright-owens-b4ab2915*

www.ingramcontent.com/pod-product-compliance
Lightning Source LLC
Chambersburg PA
CBHW060844260726
48661CB00002B/591